NIYI OSUNDARE was born in Ikẹrẹ-Ekiti, Nigeria, in 1947.
He studied English Literature for his BA degree at the
University of Ibadan, Nigeria, and followed this up with an
MA from the University of Leeds and a PhD from York
University, Toronto. He has taught at the University of Ibadan
since 1974. From 1990–91 he was Fulbright Scholar and
Writer-in-Residence at the University of Wisconsin, Madison.
He is currently Visiting Associate Professor of African and
Caribbean Literature at the University of New Orleans. He is a
columnist for *Newswatch*, Nigeria's premier news magazine,
and also for the *Sunday Tribune*, which has featured his own
poetry column since 1985. He is a frequent contributor to
West Africa. He is the first Chairperson of the Association of
Nigerian Authors, Oyo State Branch.

Osundare was awarded the Commonwealth Poetry Prize in
1986, the Association of Nigerian Authors Poetry Prize in
1986, the Cadbury Poetry Prize in 1989 and the NOMA award
in 1991.

NIYI OSUNDARE

SELECTED POEMS

HEINEMANN

Heinemann International Literature and Textbooks
A division of Heinemann Educational Books Ltd
Halley Court, Jordan Hill, Oxford OX2 8EJ

Heinemann Educational Books Inc
361 Hanover Street, Portsmouth, New Hampshire, 03801, USA

Heinemann Educational Books (Nigeria) Ltd
PMB 5205, Ibadan
Heinemann Educational Boleswa
PO Box 10103, Village Post Office, Gaborone, Botswana

LONDON   EDINBURGH   PARIS   MADRID
ATHENS   BOLOGNA   MELBOURNE
SYDNEY   AUCKLAND   SINGAPORE   TOKYO

First published by Heinemann International Literature and Textbooks in 1992

Series Editor: Adewale Maja-Pearce

British Library Cataloguing in Publication Data
A catalogue record for this book is available from the British Library.

ISBN 0 435 91195 3

PR
9387.9
.0866
A6
1992

Phototypeset by Wilmaset Ltd, Wirral
Printed and bound in Great Britain
by Cox and Wyman Ltd, Reading, Berkshire

92 93 94 95 10 9 8 7 6 5 4 3 2 1

47993

CONTENTS

For

Chief Tayo Olaitan Ayodele
Brother
Teacher
Pioneering Spirit

who piloted these dreams
through dawn's murky waters
and taught me abiding lessons
in love and generosity

A NIB
IN THE
POND

The Word

is a pod
quick with unspoken seeds
exploding in the dry season
of occasion

is an egg
broken,
it spreads
ungatherably

ear's food
mind's nurture
router of silences
sun of noons of action

Calling a Spade

No need hiding
in the tabernacle of words
so easily swept off
by the storm of anger

No need camouflaging
behind a flimsy jungle
of occult id-ioms
the metaphor of protest
flips every leaf
in the book of change

Spade callers they are
who till the fertilest terrains
for the richest harvests
knowing as they do that

the simple word
is the shortest distance
between two minds

There is no petname for
injustice
Poverty
        has no bank for nicknames.

The Poet

is not a gadfly
stinging putrefying carcasses
a
lone
in garbage lanes
no closet ink
can wash soiled streets
without the detergent
of collective action

is not a maverick
self-
consciously
deaf
to the homing whistle
through frayed jeans
can be seen, threadbare,
the flimsy texture
of feigning rebels

is not a prophet,
God's hollow ventriloquist,
auguring past futures
in dated tongues
the poet's eyes are washed
in the common spring
though seeing beyond
the hazy horizon
of lowering skies

The poet's pen is
the cactus by the stream
(shorn of its forbidding thorns)
each stem a nib
towards the field of action
its sap the ink of succour
when doubt's drought
assaults the well

Who says the poet
should leave the muck
unraked?
in a land of choking mud
how can the poet
strut
clean
in feathered sandals
and
pretend to the world
he never smells?

Shaping Clay

Make me your clay
and shape me
shape me to your heart's content
baby me in your moulding palms
their lines birthmarks
on my supple back
and when your potter's will is done
wean me off to your emboldening kiln

Make me your seed
and plant me
plant me in the lush valley
of your loamy bosom
and on the fifth day
watch my bladesome sprout
cut through the dewy shyness of earth
watch me tame stubborn weeds
watch me bloom your barn
with bounteous harvests

Make me your song
and sing me
sing me clean and clear
like a whistle
mind my matter, mould my manner
for what is the song
without the singing
the singing
without the song?

Sing me
in temples and taverns
in bedchambers and marketplaces
in farmlands and factory floors
in GRAs[1] and sprawling slums

Shape me
Plant me
Sing me

To wake a slumbering world.

[1]*GRAs* Government Reserved Areas (exclusive, privileged)

Like the Bee

(after Francis Bacon)

Not like the spider
draping crowded rooms
in the wanton web
of flimsy looms
a welter of legs spinning
silky bridges, fragile,
for the empty feet of air

Not like the wood-insect
carpentering logs to fashion
its own prison
stockaded pupae peeping
behind bars of enslaving labour

But like the bee
brewing one honey
from the nectars
of several seasons
pleasing the bud
of every clime.

Not Standing Still

I grew weary of the tyranny of water
and spat in the sea
I grew wary of the power of the sun
and lit candles at noon

A juicy rodent ran across
my morning path
I aimed my water-pot
at its teasing head
the quarry mocked
the potsherds of my lust
but it didn't go
without a dripping tail

Not standing still
is the beginning of battle
he will never pluck the fruit
whose back caresses the earth

The circle which has a beginning
also has an end
a little patience is what it needs
the stammerer will call
his father's name.

A Nib in the Pond

We read your lines
opening up the earth
like a book of paths
hear your voice
melting the wax of a thousand seasons

You who throw a nib
in the pond of silence
the ripples in your inkpot
convulse barracks and powerbrothels
overturning plots of plunder
lying on calculating tables
like poison bowls

We sing the lines
and hear our voice
read the words
and see ourselves
in the mirror of every letter

Now
though hands are two
we know which wipes the anus
there is a fork in the road
but we know the shorter way home.

Scribbling Hoe

The farmer
pens the pages of earth
with the nib
of a forge-fresh hoe
scribbles mounds
between margins of blooming corn
cursives paragraphs of legumes
in ruled furrows
his barn is a library
of nourishing seasons

Questions for a Pandering Poet

What is the poet doing
in the corridors of power:

romping to the ravaging rumblings
of constipated stomachs

nodding to the killsome lies
of reptiles of state

swaying to the rustling silk
of state fops

festering on the sputumed remains
of political tables

clapping for the airy ramblings
of ghosted tirades

peeping at the eunuch beds
of noisy chambers

licking the bloodied boots
of goose steppers?

Of man and mammon
duty and diadem
nous and nescience
who still argues
which side the poet should be?

Atewolara[1]

(for Tunde Odunlade)

We have teemed in desert temples
crawled in mystery mosques
mumbling carrion of forgotten tongues

We have swarmed shrinking shrines
of skeletal gods
and altars weighted down
by termites of faith

Reared as we are
to take life
as a knotty theorem
of unarguable givens

And cry the people:
Who shall save us?

Who shall save us
from a sea red with death's threat
and the armed legion
of mercedesed Pharaohs?

Then
came a whisper
urgent like harmattan finger
prompting like a prick:

[1]*Atewolara*   the hand is the best companion

wake you up
and befriend your mind
you will see the answers
permanenced in the lines
of your palm

Letter from the Publisher

Please find herewith
your manuscript returned
sorry we do not publish
unknown writers.

For John Donne

Hopping from bed to bed
like a bug irrepressibly on heat
your roving songs crumpled a thousand sheets
parting trilling lips in seminal closets

Loving, your love songs
penetrating like a barbed baton
conceived *new found landes* and Americas
solemnized marriages in bug bellies

Every metaphor sweats
from the orgasmic gasps
of fallopian journeys

                    Then
your compass legs (now trousered)
completed the circle
womansong mellowed into godsong
the altar jilted the bed

Jack to John, Donne to Dean
Don Juan to John Donne

O metaphor of merry metamorphosis!

Promise Land

Should we should we not pray
for them who thunder promises
from prefab podiums
feeding famished ears with vows
of promise lands

Should we should we not pray
for them who banish thought
from action
murder reason, exile hope
hang poets for their dreams
claiming every right to think
without a mind

Should we should we not pray
by their bedside
who ravish our future
in castles sentried
by brass buttons and eunuch cannon

Should we should we not pray
for them who scorch our sun
matchet our moon
ordering us to greet
with bugles and drums
the majesty of their power

?   ?   ?   ?

Arise
you for so long crushed
under the elephant's weight

We shall reach the promised land
through the wilderness of our palm.

The Warrior of Change

(*for Balarabe Musa*)

Straight
when devious paths crook the forest
and crabprints confuse sands
in eyeless scramble

        you are *iroko*[1]
        amid a thicket of swaying bamboos

Stead fast
when power carrots crush
the abstinence of will
and baits breed belches
in the moving bowels
of power pimps

        you are an uncommon firmness
        in an era that profits by shift

Clear
when goldcoated tongues
drivel doubletalk
racked on a sintax of ruse

        your unwavering words
        leave no loopholes
        in an age which seeks alibi
        in the slippery labyrinth of words

Baffled, they ask:
how can a warrior of change
battle rabid dinosaurs
leeched to the tail of time;
how jolt a conscience
mired in moribund custom?

And you say:
through a clash of wills
so powerful the sparks
radiate yester-errors
that misform our present
sparks so powerful
they illuminate the paths
so our forward march
no longer stumbles
on pyramids of oppression

After this haze
we shall see the face of the sun
for you have looked at the sky
and seen beyond the clouds.

[1]*iroko*   large tree found in the rainforest; also called 'the African oak'

Collage

Only one brief night
and a bride becomes a wife

*

Fancying millionaires
without trampled scruples
is like imagining omelettes
without shattered shells

*

Comrades or come-raids
trail-blazers or blaze-trailers
damask or the mask

*

For every finger you point
three others are arrows
towards your heart

*

Hail liberals
who give with the left
and take with the right

*

Be a good citizen:
don't argue

*

From praying ground to preying ground
from democracy to demoncrazy
from conscience to con- science

*

Waste time
and a wound becomes a sore

*

We demand justice
they give us judgement

*

If you turn the world
into a lake of poison
you will drink a bowl

*

Allies or all lies
adultery or adult tree
message or mess age

*

Heathrow finger in immigrant panties
Virginity test in a fair free isle

*

When the pestle fights the mortar
It is the yam that suffers

*

The sky
Is our village umbrella:
If you tear the portion
Above your roof,
There will be rain-water
In my inner rooms

*

All that glitters
Has to be gold

*

One two three four
Let's end the Arms Race
Not end the Human Race

*

Curse me
with a gentle eye
Damn me
with a nod
Sting me
with a stunning smile

*

After you
there will be no blank pages
in my book of memory

*

Nuclear clouds
have no silver lining

I am the Common Man

I
am the sturdiest plank
in a campaign platform
stamped countless times
to pound lies into a dough of deceit.

I
am the base element
in the chemistry of numbers
added
subtracted
multiplied
at will
in the politics of fractions

I
am a housing problem
depression agent
for whom the Vagrancy Act
was lobbied into being

I
who put the foam
in the soapbox
fire in the thunder
of close-fisted harangues

I
am the toast
in every palace
the dessert
of royal belches

But
I am truly
the flower of the forest
the salt of the sea
the sun of the sky
the wheel of a moving world

Unfellable
like a tree with a million roots
I will shake the earth
with giant fruits
lading the four winds
with seeds of change.

Noon Yet

(for Femi Ogunmola)

I didn't pluck my flowers
too early in the forest
so they do not droop
with lengthening shadows

I didn't cook my yam
in the pot of night
so its flavour doesn't perish
before the waking mouth

I will not shout out myself
before the festival of songs
so a frog of excess
doesn't jump into my eager throat

He who listens well
will hear the footsteps of ants
he who probes the bloom
will hear fragrances of vanished gardens

If I live long enough
I will eat meat
the size of a thousand elephants
my teeth all ivory, my dusk a golden feast

Time it may take
time it may take
the raw yam will turn
a smiling morsel

Time it may take
the stammerer will
one day pronounce
his father's name

THE EYE
OF THE
EARTH

Earth

Temporary basement
and lasting roof

first clayey coyness
and last alluvial joy

breadbasket
and compost bed

rocks and rivers
muds and mountains

silence of the twilight sea
echoes of the noonsome tide

milk of mellowing moon
fire of tropical hearth

spouse of the roving sky
virgin of a thousand offsprings

Ọgẹ́ẹ́rẹ́ amọ́kọ́yẹrĭ[1]

---

[1] *Ọgẹ́ẹ́rẹ́ amọ́kọ́yẹrĭ*   the one that shaves his head with the hoe

from Forest Echoes

(*with flute and heavy drums*)

A green desire, perfumed memories,
a leafy longing lure my wanderer feet
to this forest of a thousand wonders.
A green desire for this petalled umbrella
of simple stars and compound suns.
Suddenly, so soberly suddenly,
the sky is tree-high
and the horizon dips into an inky grove
like a masquerade scribbling loric fear
in the lines of festival streets.

> The rains have kept their time this year
> (Earth has (finally) won the love of the sky)
> Trees bob with barkward sap
> and leaves grab a deepening green
> from the scanty sun.

Bouncing boughs interlock overhead
like wristwrestlers straining muscularly
on a canvas of leaves wounded
by the fists of time
I tread, soft-soled, the compost carpet
of darkling jungles
my nose one charmed universe
of budding herbs and ripening roots
I tread the compost carpet of darkling forests
where terror grows on trembling leaves
natured by lore
nurtured by fairy truths

Here, under this awning, ageless,
the clock, unhanded, falls
in the deep belly of woods
its memory ticking songfully
in *elulu*'s[1] sleepless throat
Mauled the minutes, harried the hours;
taunted is time whose needle's eye
gates our comings and goings
time which wombed the moon
to bear the sun,
the hole in the ragged wardrobe
the gap in the ageing teeth
the bud on the ripening tree
Oh time,
coffin behind the cot.

And every toemark on the footpath
every fingerprint on every bark
the ropy climbers flung breathlessly
from tree to tree
the haunting sound and silence
of this sweet and sour forest
dig deep channels to the sea of memory.
And the outcome:
       will it be flow or flood . . .

---

[1] *elulu* bird which sings at regular times of the day; also called the time-keeper bird

The Rocks Rose to Meet Me

I
(*To be chanted with agba drum throbbing in the background*)

The rocks rose to meet me
like passionate lovers on a long-awaited tryst.
The rocks rose to meet me
their peaks cradled in ageless mists.
Olosunta[1] spoke first
the eloquent one
whose mouth is the talking house of ivory
Olosunta spoke first
the lofty one whose eyes are
balls of the winking sun
Olosunta spoke first
the riddling one whose belly is wrestling ground
for god and gold.

'You have been long, very long, and far,'
said he, his tongue one flaming flash
of unburnable gnomes
'Unwearying wayfarer,
your feet wear the mud of distant waters
your hems gather the bur
of fartherest forests;
I can see the westmost sun
in the mirror of your wandering eyes.'

---

[1] *Olosunta* a huge, imposing rock in Ikẹre, worshipped yearly during
the popular *Olosunta* festival; reputed to be a repository of gold

So saying, he smiled
the trees swaying their leafy heads
in the choreography of his moving lips
so saying, the sun lifted the wrinkle of clouds
from the face of a frowning sky.

Olosunta spoke first
the elephant hand which hits the haughty man in the
head
and his testicles leak to the wondering earth
like overripe *oro* fruits in a thunderstorm
Olosunta spoke
his belly still battle ground of god and gold.
The god I have killed
since wisdom's straightening sun
licked clean the infant dew of fancy
The gold let us dig,
not for the gilded craniums
of hollow chieftains
(time's undying sword awaits their necks
who deem this earth their sprawling throne).
With the gold let us turn hovels into havens
paupers into people (not princes)
so hamlets may hear
the tidings of towns
so the world may sprout a hand
of equal fingers.

Yield your gold, lofty one.
But how dig the gold
without breaking the rock?

II

Oroole[1] came next
his ancient voice tremulous
in the morning air
(harmattans here whip with the flaying fury
of a slavemaster,
but how can we banish them
without a season of unripened peas?)

Pyramid of the brood,
you who rob your head to pay your foot:
for earth is where we stand
earth is where we strive,
and what greater vantage to a wrestling rock
than a platform of a thousand feet?

Behold, cornfields flourish around your foot
elephant grass fallows the land
for unborn harvests.
Swell the grain
with living water from your rocky arteries,
fatten the tuber,
so the hoe does not scoop a sterile clod
so the dibble does not drill a defeaned dross.
Pyramid of the brood
whose unclosing eyes witness
every stroke and every dot at *Amoye*.[2]
You who loomed so fearsomely close
in the harmattan dawns of our learning days

[1] *Oroole*   a pyramid-shaped rock, also in Ikẹrẹ
[2] *Amoye*   Amoye Grammar School, sited under the shadows of *Oroole*

35

before withdrawing into stony distance
with the noonward sun.

III

The rocks rose to meet me
Tall rocks, short rocks
sharp rocks, round rocks:
some with the staid steps
of war-wise warriors
others with the gaysome gaits
of pandering pilgrims.

The rocks rose to meet me
eloquent in their deafening silence.
The rocks rose
their shadows a robe
of ungatherable hems

IV
(*The drums quieting*)

I saw the invisible toe-marks
of Esidale
indelible on the spine-less column
of rocks
unrubbable like a birthmark
older than God
hieroglyphed when earth was molten pap
sculpted into stone by the busy hands
of wind and water.

I saw toe-marks
which laked the rain
for the waiting sun
thirsty like a Sahara camel
I read the cipher tattooed
on the biceps of stone
open like a book of oracles.

The rocks rose to meet me
their legs lithesome with lithic lore.
At every step the earth shook
like an ancient deck
trees trembled from roof to root.
The rocks rose to meet me
with ankle-bells of ploding pods
and seeds scattered like a million beads.
The rocks rose to meet my wanderer eyes
singing songs of sunken suns and worsted winds:

> with such defiant brows
> with such unfurrowed faces

just what have the rains been doing?

Harvestcall

I
(To be chanted to lively bata music)

This is Iyañfọwọ́rọgi
where, garnished in green
pounded yam rested its feted arms
on the back of stooping stakes.
This is Iyañfọwọ́rọgi
where valiant heaps cracked, finally,
from the unquenchable zeal of fattening yams.

This is Iyañfọwọ́rọgi
where yams, ripe and randy,
waged a noisy war against the knife;
here where, subdued by fire,
efùrù[1] provoked mouthful clamour
from the combat of hungry wood:
>the pestle fights the mortar
>the mortar fights the pestle
>a dough of contention smooths down
>the rugged anger of hunger

Here where yam wore the crown
in the reign of swollen roots
amid a retinue of vines and royal leaves;
between insistent sky and yielding earth,
the sun mellowed planting pageants
into harvest march,
a fiery pestle in his ripening hand.

[1] *efùrù* the king of yams

this is Iyanfoworogi
where a tempting yam sauntered
out of the selling tray
and the marketplace became a mob
of instant suitors.

II

And this Òkè Ènìjù
where coy cobs rocked lustily
in the loin of swaying stalks.
Once here in May
a tasselled joy robed the field
like hemless green.
Once here in May
the sky was a riot of pollen grains
and ivory mills waited (im)patiently
for the browning of grey tassels.

And when June had finally grabbed the year
by her narrow waist
corn cobs flashed their milky teeth
in disrobing kitchens.
Plenty's season announced its coming
and the humming mill at dawn
suddenly became the village heart.

III

(Finally) Ògbèsè Odò
where cotton pods, lips duly parted
by December's sun,
draped busy farmsteads

in a harvest of smiles.
Here a blooming loom curtailed
the tiger claws of the harmattan
and earth's wardrobe lent a garb
to every season.

IV
(*Music lowers in tempo, becoming solemn*)

But where **are** they?
Where are they gone:
aróso, fèrègèdè, òtíílí, pàkalà[1]
which beckoned lustily to the reaping basket
Where are they
the yam pyramids which challenged the sun
in busy barns
Where are they
the pumpkins which caressed earthbreast
like mammary burdens
Where are they
the pods which sweetened harvest air
with the clatter of dispersing seeds?
Where are they? Where are they gone?

Uncountable seeds lie sleeping
in the womb of earth
uncountable seeds
awaiting the quickening tap
of our waking finger.
With our earth so warm
How can our hearth be so cold?

[1] *aróso, fèrègèdè, òtíílí, pàkalà* all four are types of beans

Let Earth's Pain be Soothed

(for the one who brought rainy news from Under-the-Rock)

(to the accompaniment of a flute and/or the rain drum)

The sky carries a boil of anguish
Let it burst

Our earth has never lingered so dry
in the season of falling showers
clouds journey over trees and over hills
miserly with their liquid treasure

The sky carries a boil of anguish
Let it burst

Prostrate like famished horses
brown hills cast vacant looks
at balded plains where playing kids
provoke the dust in what once was
the cradle of green

The sky carries a boil of anguish
Let it burst

Dust
dust in brewing kitchens
dust in eating halls
dust in busy bedrooms
dust in scheming boardrooms
dust in retrenching factories
dust in power brothels

The sky carries a boil of anguish
Let it burst

Let it rain today
    that parched throats may sing
Let it rain
    that earth may heal her silence
Let it rain today
    that cornleaves may clothe the hills
Let it rain
    that roots may swell the womb of lying plains
Let it rain today
    that stomachs may shun the rumble of thunder
Let it rain
    that children may bath and bawl and brawl

The sky carries a boil of anguish
Let it burst

The roofs have been silent too long
the seeds noiseless in the dormitory of the soil
the earth has been lying too long, and songless.

Time to leap, time to lilt

Let the sky's boil of anguish burst today
The pain of earth be soothed.

First Rain

a tingling tang awakes the nose
when the first rain has just clipped
the wing of the haughty dust
a cooling warmth embraces
our searching soles
as the land vapour rises
like a bootless infantry

and
through her liberated pores
     our earth breathes again.

Raindrum

The roofs sizzle at the waking touch,
talkative like kettledrums
tightened by the iron fingers of drought

Streets break into liquid dance
gathering legs in the orchestra of the road
Streets break into liquid dance
gliding eloquently down the apron of the sky

A stray drop saunters down the thatch
of my remembrance
waking memories long dormant
under the dry leaves of time:

> of caked riverbeds
> and browned pastures
> of baking noons
> and grilling nights
> of earless cornfields
> and tired tubers

Then
Lightning strikes its match of rain
Barefoot, we tread the throbbing earth.

Renewed

Meet me at Okeruku

Meet me at Òkèrukù[1]
where earth is one compact
of reddening powder
daubed coquettishly
on the harmattan brow
of trembling houses

And when the rains are here
when this dust is clod and clay
show me your camwood shoes
show me hurried toemarks
on the ciphered pages of narrow alleys
awaiting the liquid erazer
of the next shower

---

[1] *Òkèrukù*   a red-earth district in Ikẹrẹ

But Sometimes when it Rains

But sometimes when it rains
and an angry thunder raps earth's ears
with its hands of fire
Sometimes when it rains
and a heartless storm beheads
the poor man's house
like some long-convicted felon.

      Sometimes when it rains
      you wonder who sent the skies weeping

Sometimes when it rains
and an impregnable mahogany falls
across your farmward path
sometimes when it rains
and a streamlet swollen with watery pride
drowns your fields and tender tubers

      Sometimes when it rains
      you wonder who sent the skies weeping

Sometimes when it rains
and a diligent tryst is washed out
by a careless downpour
sometimes when it rains
and a callous mist thickens
between you and the waiting one
sometimes when it rains
dreams are wet with the desperate longing
of a jilted embrace

You wonder who sent the skies weeping
sometimes when it rains.

Farmer-born

Farmer-born peasant-bred
I have frolicked from furrow to furrow
sounded kicking tubers in the womb
of quickening earth
and fondled the melon breasts
of succulent ridges.

Farmer-born peasant-bred
I have traced the earthworm's intricate paths
on the map of dawn
heeded dew-call to the upland farm
and, sun-sent, have sought *iroko*[1] refuge
at hungry noons.

Farmer-born peasant-bred
I have lived on the aroma
of fresh-felled forests
relished the delicious symmetry
of *akee apple*[2] colours
and plucked the pendulous promise of ripening
pawpaw

Farmer-born peasant-bred
I have rattled the fleshy umbrella
of mushroom jungles
rustled the compost carpet of fallen leaves
and savoured the songful clatter
of opening pods

Farmer-born peasant-bred
classroom-bled
I have thrown open my kitchen doors
and asked hunger to take a seat,
my stomach a howling dump
for Carolina rice.

[^1]: *iroko*   large tree found in the rainforest; also called 'the African oak'
[^2]: *akee apple*   tropical fruit with a pink bell-shaped pod (green when unripe), cream-white flesh, and glossy black seeds

Ours to Plough, not to Plunder

The earth is ours to plough and plant
the hoe is her barber
the dibble her dimple

Out with mattocks and matchets
bring calabash trays and rocking baskets
let the sweat which swells earthroot
relieve heavy heaps of their tuberous burdens

Let wheatfields raise their breadsome hands
to the ripening sun
let legumes clothe the naked bosom
of shivering mounds
let the pawpaw swell and swing
its headward breasts

Let water spring
from earth's unfathomed fountain
let gold rush
from her deep unseeable mines
hitch up a ladder to the dodging sky
let's put a sun in every night

Our earth is an unopened grainhouse,
a bustling barn in some far, uncharted jungle
a distant gem in a rough unhappy dust
This earth is
      ours to work not to waste
      ours to man not to maim
This earth is ours to plough, not to plunder

Our Earth will not Die

(To a solemn, almost elegiac tune)

> Lynched
>   the lakes
> Slaughtered
>   the seas
> Mauled
>   the mountains

But our earth will not die

> Here
>   there
>   everywhere
> a lake is killed by the arsenic urine
> from the bladder of profit factories
> a poisoned stream staggers down the hills
> coughing chaos in the sickly sea
> the wailing whale, belly up like a frying fish,
> crests the chilling swansong of parting waters.

But our earth will not die.

> Who lynched the lakes. Who?
> Who slaughtered the seas. Who?
> Whoever mauled the mountains. Whoever?

Our earth will not die

> And the rain
> the rain falls, acid, on balding forests

their branches amputated by the septic daggers
of tainted clouds

Weeping willows drip mercury tears
in the eye of sobbing terrains
a nuclear sun rises like a funeral ball
reducing man and meadow to dust and dirt.

But our earth will not die.

Fishes have died in the waters.   Fishes.
Birds have died in the trees.   Birds.
Rabbits have died in their burrows.   Rabbits.

But our earth will not die

(*Music turns festive, louder*)

Our earth will see again
eyes washed by a new rain
the westering sun will rise again
resplendent like a new coin.
The wind, unwound, will play its tune
trees twittering, grasses dancing;
hillsides will rock with blooming harvests
the plains batting their eyes of grass and grace.
The sea will drink its heart's content
when a jubilant thunder flings open the skygate
and a new rain tumbles down
in drums of joy.
Our earth will see again

this earth, OUR EARTH.

MOONSONGS

I

(To the accompaniment of lively wọ́rọ̀ drumming, the following song, in call-and-response)

> *Pèrée o pèré yọjú l'ọ́run*
> *Àgbámùréré*
>
> *Pèrée o pèré yọjú l'ọ́run*
> *Àgbámùréré*
>
> *Àṣẹ̀ṣẹ̀yọ oṣù ó dà bí egbin*
> *Àgbámùréré*
>
> *Ká kóṣu kóbì ká lọ mú ṣaya*
> *Àgbámùréré*
>
> *Ká tó dé bẹ̀ ó ti b'ójọ́ lo*
> *Àgbámùréré*
>
> *Kírìjí kírìjí kírìjí pẹpẹlúpẹ*
> *Àgbámùréré*[1]

Spread the sky like a generous mat
Tell dozing rivers to stir their tongues
Unhinge the hills
Unwind the winds
The moon and I will sing tonight

Kírìjí kírìjí kírìjí pẹpẹlúpẹ . . .

Oh moon, matron, master, eternal maiden.
The bounce of your bosom
The miracle of your cheeks
Your smile which ripens the forests
Your frown which wrinkles the dusk

The youth of your age
The age of your youth
All, all await
The echoing thunder of my riddling chants

Kírìjí kírìjí kírìjí pẹpẹlúpẹ . . .

Let the cricket slit night's silence
With the scalpel of its throat
Let nightbirds coo and cuddle
In the swinging Eden of their nests;
But when dawn finally climbs down
Through the leering rafters,
I will be a promise
Eternal like your seasonless sky

Kírìjí kírìjí kírìjí pẹpẹlúpẹ . . .

And the moon masters the stars
Masters the sea
Sharpens every tip of its tidal teeth
Rattles every grain of its salty roost
Probes every drop of its diurnal blue
Ah! there are latitudes of sweat
On the brow of the sea;
A tropical truth taunts the waves
Surging beachwards like an armada
Of foaming sharks

Kírìjí kírìjí kírìjí pẹpẹlúpẹ . . .

Bell-ringers, the shells shout time's segments
In the dormitory of dodging depths
Heard, not hearing,

Kneaded into millennial reefs and rocks
By the distant fingers of clever water
The penguin smells the moon
In the greying hem of its clumsy coat,
The beaches chew their sands
With the gritty vigour of rootless teeth

Kírìjí kírìjí kírìjí pẹpẹlúpẹ . . .

New-sprung from the tabernacle of iron clouds,
The moon is a wandering sickle
Of gathering vows
With a dialect of whispers, covenant of simmering sighs:
The gallant plucks her like a fairy petal
On nights when the lanes are low
And flaming breaths tickle the ears of patient walls,
When moonmaids bathe lunar cycles in the blue mercy
Of scarlet waters
Their heads wavelocks of plaited bubbles;
Their wardrobe is mist,
Their sandals beadwork of fiery scales

Kírìjí kírìjí kírìjí pẹpẹlúpẹ . . .

Fiery scales, fiery scales
So eloquent in the manhood of the sun

Oh sea

     season

       seasun . . .

The sun which blues the sea,
Which tones its flesh,

Before chasing twilight's orange
To the fringes of distant depths

Kírìjí kírìjí kírìjí pępęlúpę . . .

Beyond the palms, beyond the paddles
Beyond shimmering limits
Where the sea hugs the sky with a liquid passion,
The moon reads sunsteps in the alphabet
Of protean sands,
The moon heals the scars of wounded winds

Kírìjí kírìjí kírìjí pępęlúpę . . .

Spread the sky
Unwind the wind
Let moonmares rein in the infinity
Of galloping hours.

Spread the sky
Unwind the wind
Let moonmirrors shape the amplitude
Of sundry strivings

*Pèrée o pèré yǫjú l'ǫrun
Àgbámùréré . . .*

---

[1] Fresh, fresh does the moon appear in the sky
   Àgbámùréré
   New moon is beautiful like a fairy
   Àgbámùréré
   Bring yams, bring kolanuts, let's go and marry her
   Àgbámùréré
   Before we get up there she has gone with Time
   Àgbámùréré

II

The moon is a mask dancing
               mask dancing
               mask dancing

The moon is a mask dancing

And in the milky grove
between the cloudmountains
the moon's tropical eyes
are chameleons of silver forests

The moon is a mask dancing

Her lips coiled
like corridors of a thousand snakes
breathing hot, breathing cold
lilting labial lyrics of tangled nights
Oh moon, mother me in the surging valley
of your knowing bosom:
there are clanging armours
in the aprons of the forest,
twilight clears a throat of bleeding spears,
     let dawn clip the tongue of murdering drums
     let dawn clip the tongue of murdering drums

The moon is a mask dancing

And in the tempered peace which rustles
the dew of nodding forests,
in the silence which fore-goes
the gallop of fertile thunders

let me see your voice
so lithe, so light, like eggs of starsparrows
    I will not let fall the eggs
    I will not let the eggs fall

The moon is a mask dancing

III

*I must be given words to refashion futures
like a healer's hand*

   Edward Kamau Brathwaite

We called the statue
To a talking feast
Before knowing the chisel
Never left a tongue in its rigid mouth . . .

   From the silence of the seasons
   From the hush which murdered the wind
   With thunder's sword
   We borrow the restless throat of *àdòko*[1]
   We borrow the permanent query
   On the parrot's beclamoured beak

From the vowel of the river
From the consonant of striving valleys
We name the moon, we name the sun
We pledge a fluent chatter to the stammering sea

From seasons which pass but never part
I borrow moonbeams to shape the wind.

[1]*àdòko*   a bird noted for incessant songs

V

Frantic as a prentice poet
the young moon unfolds,
a wickless lamp
in the silence of lingering nights

trees preen their tops
walls unplug their ears
and hills advance,
minding every crater
on memory's road

moonrays have flared into song
the ballad sizzles in the chimney
of crooning noses;
stars red up the sky
with echoes of silver breaths

can it smell the echo, can it see the chant
a sky whose ears are sealed
by the wax of waning moons?

can it hear
when syllables thrum angry triggers
and consonants fall from heaven
like a hail of vengeful scorpions?

like a troubador
the moon unfolds her songs
by dusty roadsides of the sky;
the moon unfolds her songs
nomadic like a restless truth

VI

Night after night
the wind spreads out the sky

And the moon, too busy to sleep,
snatches fleeting dreams in tunnels
of nodding clouds,
swaying so solemnly to the summon
        of the drum
            of the drum
so loud now with the membrane of the sun

And with its rhythm of rocks
memory of meadows
hieroglyph of hills
with its ding-dong of dawn-and-dusk
the moon lilts and laughs,
a millennial tear standing hot
in the amplitude of its eye

The tear bursts into brook
ripens into river
then gallops like a liquid mare
towards the sea

All at dawn
when the moon is a seasoned navel
in the stomach of the sky.

X

Tell me, moon,
Where are your wrecks
Where are your wrinkles
Where, the creases left
On your wondrous robe
By the crow-foot fury
Of the wandering wind?

The tendril plies the seasons
And reaps the sponge,
The river's hot-browed swagger
In the empire of the mountain
Softens so slowly into the mellow commonwealth
Of the spreading coast;
The universe sows its minutes, reaps its hours:
Grey strands run their course on the bristling asphalt
Of cruising dreams.

Ashes are the echo of fire
The nose is the memory of the face
The drum is an open hint of a hide
That loved its flesh

The universe sows its minutes, reaps its hours.

And in those moments of joyous ripening
When green turns gold and gold melts
Into phantoms of wizened silver
Ticking mountains fine-ally strike their hour
And the world quakes with streaks of solar depths

Beyond the wilderness of stone
Beyond valleys of suffocating veils
Beyond Wednesdays of unpenitent ash
A Monday flings open the door of the week,
A pliant clay in its waking hand:
Supple moments, oh supple moments!
And brittle breaths unchain the dance
And ample hands unhush the drum
Not even the salt of the sea, so bitter
With foams of epileptic scars
Not even the deciduous hustle of declining herbs
Can grey this dappled dream
So gently planted in the temple of our sleep
The universe which sows its minutes
Will reap its hours

XII

(for Joan Rayfield, tenderer of fertile cultures)

Moonfire too is deciduous;
its conifers weep their leaves
like yellow tears;

And in the dappled darings
of autumn
when yearning winds press lyrical lips
on the apple's demurring bosom,
skyfields are sweaty tracks
for the garnerer's unwavering feet

There is a golden chatter
in the bowers of busy barns
the air leans low with the fragrance
of active ripening;
moonchildren plod skyways
with baskets of mellowed vows
and the stars are heavy pods
of jolly juice

And the seasons which stirred the sod
which hoed the humus
when moonfields were green elves
sprouting from a vibrant wilderness of lunar pores;
those seasons, where are they now,
this moment of delicious shadows?

Iṣẹ́ lòṣùpá ńṣe lálède ọ̀run, lálède ọ̀run
Iṣẹ̀ lòṣùpá ńṣe . . .[1]

But good old Armstrong
in his weightless walk,
did he trample moonharvests
in the science of green visions?

---

[1] Busy is the moon in the compound of the sky
  Busy is the moon

XVI

Now I know why the caged bird sings
Why the caged bird sings
Why the caged bird sings
Now I know why the caged bird sings
When the Moon is a knot of strings

The slope of night finally loiters
through the convex cornea of the sky;
and silence rakes up the streets
with epaulettes of terror

Now I know why the caged bird sings

A kiwi-ed boot traps a star
in a regimented shimmer
the skybird flips and flaps
as a cagey night now turns
a galaxy of sweating feathers

Now I know why the caged bird sings

Why the caged bird sings
Why the caged bird sings
Why the caged bird chants every note
on the saddle of crawling hours
when swagger sticks twine into
blustering vipers in the trembling squares
of our gathering fears
patriarchs who plough the word
are snake-charmers now
in the streetcorner of our dreams

Now I know why the caged bird sings

The General missiles a swagger
and a nest of edicts jets out
of his adamantine mouth . . .
The general is up, up, up
The general is up
There is a beltful of scars
In the furrows of our sweating backs

Now I know why the caged bird sings

Night
when minutes goose-step
in barracks of golden eggs,
the barrel of the gun ever so smooth
with crudes of petroleum rackets

Now I know why the caged bird sings

Why the caged bird sings
Why the caged bird sings
The night ticks on like a giant clock;
and the young moon eyes its infant watch:
Dawn will not be long
Dawn will not be long
Then shall we all know

Why the caged bird sings.

XVII

The lion borrows its name
from the eloquence of its mane;
the forest's *oríki*[1]
is the green syllable
of towering trees.

And what dumb gold
when drought has mined the leaves
and the birds, voiceless vagrants,
drift, drift, north with their baggage of songs?

The world is a mask dancing
            mask dancing
            mask dancing
Every agile sole knows the sizzling symphony
of the winged dust.

There is a fleeting flock
in the pasture of the moon:
the shepherd senses his twilight
in the static mirror of the eye of the sheep

The rain fell in June
and December licked it brown
with its feline tongue:
they who marvel the sinews of our dust
let them ask what happened to the offsprings
of our yester-showers

The rain is going going going
like a long-besotted bride

But if the sun drags the river
into its scorching harem,
can it lift the sands
from the armpit of earth?

The world is a mask dancing

<hr>

[1]*oríkì* a praisename

XIX

A madding moon
has sold the stars
sold the rocks
there is a bickering banter

in the budget of the sky.
The moon plundered the gold
drained the diamonds
and bartered its silvery ore

to the merchants of night
whose claws are cold
whose teeth are crowded tusks
of the ivory of our dreams

The moon has felled the forests
laundered the lakes
harassed the hills:
a yellowing chill stalks

the steps of lunar magnates.
The moon borrows a bullion from Mars
pawns hapless moonchildren to Jupiter;
and when skysages challenge

the dimness of the deeds
the moon pleads its sword,
pleads the bayonet tongue
of its eager guns

Now the moon has crowned our silence
gripped our songs
laid a frenzied ambush
for the syllable of our sooth

A madding moon
has sold the stars . . .
and when a wounded thunder
seeks the sanctity of the skies

Ah! the moon, the moon
will be one rotting pumpkin
in the fringes
of a smoking dawn.

XXII

Ikoyi[1]

> The moon here
> is a laundered lawn
> its grass the softness of infant fluff;
> silence grazes like a joyous lamb,
> doors romp on lazy hinges
> the ceiling is a sky
> weighted down by chandeliers
> of pampered stars

Ajegunle[1]

> here the moon
> is a jungle,
> sad like a forgotten beard
> with tensioned climbers
> and undergrowths of cancerous fury:
> cobras of anger spit in every brook
> and nights are one long prowl
> of swindled leopards

The moon is a mask dancing . . .

[1]*Ikoyi* and *Ajegunle*   areas in Lagos

XXIV

think of our eyes
sharing one sky

Joseph Bruchac: '*Awatawesu*'

Gather your hems now
Unfurl your shadows
Tell your fairy feet the road is waiting
Time for that last dance across
The threshold of the swaying sky

    Softly softly
    Softly sways the masquerade of the seasons

Unflinching brow, you who once lit up
The temple of the sky,
Golden pumpkin now in the furnace of dawn,
You have kindled the comb of the cock
Lending rising eaves their mysty trumpet

    Softly softly
    Softly sways the masquerade of the seasons

Across silver continents
Across oceans of rippling dust
Beyond deciduous discs of winking groves
Beyond tall chronicles of whispering depths
Across silence, beyond the superstition of the sea

    Softly softly
    Softly sways the masquerade of the seasons

Across the gripping muse-ic of the waking grass
In the throbbing cadence of busy nests
From the ancient chamber of patient drums
Songs ripen the foetus of the day
A misty rhapsody clears the throat of yawning dawns

    Softly softly
    Softly sways the masquerade of the seasons

The palm tenderly pledges its wine
To the parting queen,
The lake throws up its favourite fish
The hill gently yields its eloquent echo
Trees wave their leaves like bewitching fans

    Softly softly
    Softly sways the masquerade of the seasons

Behold the blue distance of prancing mountains
Behold the mellow magic of romping clouds
Behold the fairy laughter of homing maidens
With baskets of stars, garlands of crispy suns
Behold the amplitude which teases the edge of beaming
                                  skies

    Softly softly
    Softly sways the masquerade of the seasons

Quiet now the fancy of the forge
Dew-drenched, the tongue of seminal fires
Quiet now the dialect of the adze
Mist-mobbed, the prattle of the hoe
Quiet, quiet the pod of stirring seeds

    Softly softly
    Softly sways the masquerade of the seasons.

Monday Morning

(at Ibadan University)

staccato syntax
of metalled heels
confounding clamour
of sartorial colours
and
per..fumes loud-
er than waterfalls

Oh what frantic resurrection
after the festive golgotha
of passionate saturdays!
what painless awakening
after the red-light gethsemane
of crisbo gardens[1]

and then
the dozing galilee
of lecture rooms
the seraphic snore
in library carrels . . .

monday morning
week's january
when doors slammed
on stubborn sins
await the sledge hammer
of dire fridays

[1]*Crisbo Gardens*   a popular nightclub in Ibadan

Noonview

the laughing sun
    unties

the knot of quibbling birds
in their feathery parliament
below the trees . . .

      a fiery edict has sealed
      the larynx of the lyre
      And the forest leaps into green lores
      of song and rage:
      'Truth banners, truth banners,
      should they ever bear
      the banner of truth?'

*   *   *

Ruthless as a jealous artist
a raging wind wrinkles up
the garment of the forest
      every line a furrow
      on a grudging brow,
      every vein a streak
      of sneaky oaths

*   *   *

. . . and memory which breaks
the teeth of the grave . . .
      what happens to the snail
      which left its shell
      in the lengthy crevice of an absent rock?
      what hint, the mouth

which lost its tongue
in the labyrinth of the throat?

Ah! the giant stands in the rid-
dling sun
but cannot see his musing shadow

Cannot see his shadow
cannot see his shadow
rippling like a molten puzzle
in the grey truth of lengthening dusks

*   *   *

And boasts the drunken tyrant:
    'My chains are iron
    My walls are stone
    My breath is the raging fire
    Of skydragons . . .'

But death came,
not like a pounding giant
with legs of mortar,
not like a swaggering mountain
with a crown of dizzy clouds.
Death came
in the sneaky column
of meticulous rains,
in the yellow whisper
of the wind

Death came
in the stammering murmur of thunder

And . . .

Shadows of Time[1]

(*Anniversary of a future remembered*)

The clouds drift by,
nimble puppies with eyes of marble:
the sun dissolves in the hands of journeying winds
then hardens into balls of ticking stone

> I heard moonsteps in the corridors of seasons
> The sky is aflame with dusts of hurrying dials

Night melts into day melts into night
and the sun, caught between two twilights,
essays moving shadows of dew and dawn;
beyond rigid longitudes of uneven chimes
beyond alien meridians of patterned crossings
the sun bares its clocky face:
its seconds of stars, its speedy hands
playing minute pranks with pendulums of History

> I heard moonsteps in the corridors of seasons
> The sky is aflame with dusts of hurrying dials

For Time, too, has its latitudes:
the dripping rags of tumbling comets,
the lateral slit of the prompting drum
the restless spring of the heels of the egret
cruising home to hearths of chalky depths.
Ah! Time's latitude

[1]Dedicated to the 70th anniversary of *West Africa*, the London-based
news magazine in which the poem also made its first appearance

is the petulant green of the tendril
the golden prepuce of the pawpaw
the crimson song of the bleeding grave

> I heard moonsteps in the corridors of seasons
> The sky is aflame with dusts of hurrying dials

Memory's minions all:
trees reckoning rings on the ripening finger
of mating forests,
the insolent grey in the jungle of the sage's beard,
the *okro*[1] which, counting days, springs steel fibres
against the conquering knife,
those frantic dreams left in pawprints
of leonine mountains, awaiting
the levelling showers of angry clouds

> I heard moonsteps in the corridors of seasons
> The sky is aflame with dusts of hurrying dials

The harmattan looks back
    and sees the rain
the rain looks forward
    and smells the egret
Life's tides crash and crest
in the oceans of our growing eyes,
fling their fangs at the banks of our dodging dreams,
then slither seawards, a rippling python.
The tides, those tides, will come again
when the moon of our noon is crescent
above the roofs

---

[1] *okro*   a vegetable; sometimes called okra

they will come again
when the sun of our night
is hearth for our tropical strivings

    I heard moonsteps in the corridors of seasons
    The sky is aflame with dusts of hurrying dials

Time's door leans
on hinges of uncertain shores,
oiled by sooth,
dimpled by knuckles
of accumulated visions.

Keyholes here are dioramas
of purple thrones
guessed now from rusty maces
and excavated grandeurs of grey edicts.

    Time
    Time never runs its race
    Like a straight, uncluttered road
    Ah Time never does
    In Time's street are treacherous bows
    And friendly bends,
    Crucibles of 'Crucify him!',
    Alleys of Allelujahs;
    The chameleon joins eyes
    With owls of luminous nights
    But the forest still cannot see the bird
    On tomorrow's tree . . .

Time is the robe
Time is the wardrobe

Time is the needle's intricate pattern
In the labyrinth of the garment
Time is the lingering aroma
Of a long forgotten dish

    Time the seasons
    Season the times;
    The forest sprouts, blooms
    And rots into seed
    The seed mothers the mountain
    The mountain mothers the river
    And the river springs green flowers
    In Edens of unsinning apples

        I heard moonsteps in the corridors of seasons
        The sky is aflame with dusts of hurrying dials

Deciduous,
then, the smile of the moon
deciduous
the leafy fire on the brows of the sun
Time masters our steps like a general
with a thousand stars,
drills our manifold musings like a grindstone
with a thousand teeth;
we fret, we fight, we pacify mortality
with busts of stone,
monuments of loudest steel;
but the rains capture rusty chinks
in the shield of steel
storms soften stony prides into
flakes of weathered dust;
wrinkles buried so fashionably by

centuries of rosy talcum
embarrass the face after one wink
of hasty sweating . . . But

Evergreen,
Time lives in other dreams,
evergreen:
the song of the busy adze
the breath of the forge
the unfettering energy of the word,
minds touching minds touching matter

a strand of grey left in the twilight wind,
a favourite dish, a characteristic smile,
the world catches the fragrance
of our flowering visions
blooming petals of everlasting gardens

Evergreen
their breaths, who stoke the flames
of our flickering fancies

Evergreen
their winds, who lace silent echoes
with rattles of fertile thunders

Evergreen
      ever green

      I heard moonsteps in the corridors of seasons
      The sky is aflame with dusts of hurrying dials

WAITING
LAUGHTERS

Throughout, to the accompaniment of
drums, horns, and stringed instruments,
if possible the kora or goje.
Medley of voices.

I

I pluck these words from the lips of the wind
Ripe like a pendulous pledge;
Laughter's parable explodes in the groin
Of waking storms
Clamorous with a covenant
of wizened seeds

Tonalities. Redolent tonalities

Of wandering fancies yeasting into mirth,
Yeasting into glee in the crinkled lanes
Of giggling cheeks,
Lingering aroma of pungent chuckles,
The rave of ribs which spell the moments
In latitudes of tender bones

Tonalities. Redolent tonalities

I pluck these murmurs
From the laughter of the wind
The shrub's tangled tale
Plaited tree tops
And palms which drop their nuts

Like talents of golden vows
I listen solemnly to the banter
Of whistling fern
And I reap rustling rows
So fanatic in their pagan promise

Tonalities. Redolent tonalities

And laughing heels so fugitive
In the dust of fleeing truths

> Truth of the valley
> Truth of the mountain
>
> Truth of the boulder
> Truth of the river
>
> Truth of the flame
> Truth of the ash
>
> Truth of the sole
> Truth of the palm
>
> Truth of the sun
> Truth of the moon
>
> Truth of the liar
> Truth of the lair
>
> Truth of the castle
> Truth of the caste
>
> Truth of the desert
> Truth of the rain

Tonalities. Redolent tonalities

The rain. The rain
Truth of the rain's seven ingots
In the womb of the forge
And the seminal smoke which leaps

Above the roof, plodding skylanes
Before taunting thunder's raw temper
To a wild, unbridled deluge

The rain. The rain
The rain is *oníbáńbáńtibá*[1]
The rain is *oníbàńbàńtibà*
The rain which taunts the roof's dusty laughter
In the comedy of February's unsure showers;
The wind is its wing, the lake
One liquid song in its fluent concert

Tonalities. Redolent tonalities

The wind has left springing laughter
In the loins of bristling deserts;
Sands giggle in grass,
Fallowing pebbles reach for sacks of scrotal pasture

Tonalities. Redolent tonalities

And still fugitive like a fairy,
The wind gallops like a thoroughbred
Dives like a dolphin
Soars into the waiting sky
Like *àwòdì*[2] with a beak of feathery oracles

Tonalities. Redolent tonalities

[1] *oníbáńbáńtibá*   no specific semantic 'meaning'; used here as tonal
counter-point
[2] *àwòdì*   kite

88

And laughing winds
So fugitive in
Our harried seasons
        Who can tie
        Them down with
        The rope
of a single idiom   Who dare?

Tonalities. Redolent tonalities

Blame not, then,
The rapid eloquence of the running vowel
When words turn willing courier
In the courtyard of dodging ears
Can the syllable stall its tale
In impertinences of half-way fancies?

Tonalities. Redolent tonalities

I pluck these words
From the lips of running winds
When earth, yolk-yellow, clamours
For a warrant of wings
Tiptoe on the prudence of an anthill,
My covenant is clay,
Wisdom my silent wheel

Tonalities. Redolent tonalities

II

                Wait
                    ing . . .

        And the hours limp a-
        long,
        with
        band-
        ages
        of fractured moments

Every minute
heavy like an expectant rock,
the eyes labouring through
a century of winks
            And the horse gallops
            through an eternity of yawns
            through the webbed wandering
            of mangrove patience,
            in the dusty mirror
            which powders the broken mask
            of swindled deserts

            The horse gallops
            through a street which stretches
            like a rubbery code
            before slipping a criminal disc
            near the sacrum of the moon

            Then the road narrows into artery
            blossoms into egret dreams

which temper the whitened waiting
of showerless seasons

The road wanders into the street
the street wanders into the road
and road and street mellow into way,
lengthen into vision . . .

And the hours limp a-
long
longer than an April shower
longer than the cursive laughter of lightning
longer than the silk-cotton tree's mercy
in the loom of naked seasons
longer than the tortuous, broken queues
at the portals of Austerity factories!

Teach us the patience of the sand
which rocks the cradle of the river

Teach us the patience of the branch
which counts the seasons in dappled cropping

Teach us the patience of the rain
which eats the rock in toothless silence

Teach us the patience of the baobab
which tames the rage of orphaning storms

Teach us the patience of the cat
which grooms the thunder of the leaping moment

Teach us, teach us, teach us . . .

III

Waiting
> for the heifer which bides its horns
> in the womb of the calf

Waiting
> for the nail which springs an ivory wonder
> in the aprons of the finger

Waiting
> for the tome which split its spine
> in the spotted arena of reading eyes

Waiting
> for the deer which loves its hide
> and hunters who cuddle their flaying guns

Waiting
> for the razor's stubbled glide
> across the firmament of the beard

Waiting
> for fists which find their aim
> and idioms which split their atoms

> in 'ploding shadows.

IV

Waiting
> The anxious fumes of the visa awe-ffice
> thick with queries, thick with fear
> and stamps which bite trembling papers
> with purple fangs, and seals pompous
> like a mad phallus

> Narrow, the walls,
> high, imperiously white;
> the hangings stoke wondering dreams
> with their tourist havens;
> the future is one wavering complexion
> of the visaman's edict

Waiting
> in the visahouse is a chronicle of cold complaint:
> the calibrated aircon[1] coughs a chill
> in the sweaty calculations of a room
> aloud with doubt
> Exile, pilgrim, tripsters of feathered heels,
> there is a baggage of patience
> in the missionary temper of wanderlust.

> > The visaman, rightly, suited,
> > his hair correct, his parting severe,
> > takes two furtive looks at the crowded hall
> > then shuts the window with a cold,
> > imperial hiss;

The crowd's answer is a yawn,
and a few blank trips to a tired watch.

Passports are pass ports
The Atlantic is a wilderness of barbed walls
brooking no windows, its door of deafening steel

The key fell into spaceless water,
once upon a blue dragon,
then vanished, finally, into the shark's
intolerant belly.

Passports are pass ports
Knock still ye who may;
the Atlantic springs a door of deafening steel

And interrogation windows
And reluctant seats
And officers cold and clever

Like inquisitive godlings
And the metallic 'No!'
And rapid ciphers
And repatriated dreams
And wingless fancies
And darkened noons . . .

Knock still ye who may;
Seconds plod in leaden paces
in crowded visarooms.

---

[1]*aircon*   Nigerian abbreviation for air-conditioner

V

Waiting
>   like the grass honing every blade
>   for the flesh of the dew

Waiting
>   like the uncircumcised penis of okro[1]
>   peeping out of the prepuce of dawn

Waiting
>   like the lip of lettuce, the open palm of
>   ṣọkọyọ̀kọ̀tọ̀[2]
>   beckoning the sky-bound shower, beckoning

Waiting
>   like a raffia brush in the armpit of the valley,
>   iron straws on hips of dancing groves

Waiting
>   like the beard for its chin, the knee for its cap
>   the night for its day, the prayer for its amen

Waiting
>   like the forest for the umbrella of its mushroom
>   like the earth for the husband of its sky

Waiting
>   like the tyrant for his noose.

[1]*okro*   vegetable with long green pods; sometimes called okra
[2]*ṣọkọyọ̀kọ̀tọ̀*   make-the-husband-robust: a favourite Nigerian
vegetable

VI

Winnowing season: we-knowing-season
The chaff know their hell,
grains thresh a handsome pilgrimage
to the Jerusalem of the jaw;
and pumpkins unfold yellow peril
in the ripening ridges of compassionate suns

Winnowing season: we-knowing-season

'I am Croesus,' quoth he,
waiting,
his breath a gail of gold,
his swagger varnished silver of a low intemperate sky

His head asks his crown
for a humble place in its gilded castle;
the crown pulls the head by its servile hair,
then leaves it hanging like an orphaned burden

Beyond Reason, beyond Necessity
beyond Distribution which tames the Excess
of uneven mountains
beyond Virtue, beyond Need
beyond Truth which straightens the serpent
of stammering jungles
Croesus heaves a glittering crown on his head,
his neck shortening like a senile cricket's

Beyond Reason, beyond Necessity
in the orgy of crimson claws
which darken the rainbow of striving ribs
in the belly of the goblet where murdered grapes
sip their scarlet wails,
the moon, the moon, is up;
the sceptre barks its canine edict
castles crash, mortally tired of their medieval legs
waters breaking, waters breaking
royal fishes smell purple twilight
in the cemetery of baking sands

VII

Waiting
       like the Bastille, for the screaming stones
       of turbulent streets;
       their bread is stone
       their dessert garnished sand from the kitchen
       of heartless seasons
       And when the humble axe finally heeds its noble
                                 task,
       the head descends, lumpen dust in its royal mouth

       Behold the wonder;
       the crown is only a cap!

           Òrògòdodo Òrògòdo
           Òrògòdodo Òrògòdo
           Obá bá ti béyì
           Ó mò d'Òrògòdòdo o o o o[1]

       The king's brave legs are bone and flesh
       Bone and flesh, bone and flesh
       The king's brave legs are bone and flesh
       The castle is a house of mortar and stone
       Mortar and stone, mortar and stone
       A chair is wood which becomes a throne

---

[1] *Òrògòdodo Òrògòdo*
A king who dances with a dizzy swing
Òrògòdo   straight he goes

(*Òrògòdo* in Ikẹrẹ mythology is a remote place of banishment for
dishonourable rulers)

And Croesus builds a castle of strident stone.
Oh teach us the patience of the Rain
which eats the rock in toothless silence

VIII

Waiting
>on the stairs of the moon
>creaking up and down
>the milkyways of fastidious comets
>bled into speed, plucked off the vortex
>of falling flares
>my foot knows the timbre of fiery skies
>where songs still dripping
>with the sap of the wind
>dry their limbs in furnaces
>of baking proverbs
>
>My song is space
>beyond wails, beyond walls
>beyond insular hieroglyphs
>which crave the crest
>of printed waves.

IX

My song is the even rib
in the feather of the soaring bird
the pungent salt and smell of
earth
where seeds rot for roots to rise

My song is the root
touching other roots
in a covenant below the crust
beyond the roving camera of the eye

My song is the embryo of day
in the globule of the rising dew;
a vow which earths the Word
in regions of answerable rains

My song is *ògbìgbòtirigbò*[1]
waiting on the stairs of the moon
garnering lights, garnering shadows,
waiting

[1]*ògbìgbòtirigbò*   a large bird which flies high in the sky

X

The innocence of the Niger
waiting, waiting
fourhundredseasons
for the proof of the prow
waiting
for the irreverent probing of pale paddles
waiting
for the dispossessing twang of alien accents
waiting
for scrolls of serfdom, hieroglyphs of calculated
treacheries
waiting
withoutafacewithoutanamewithoutafacewithouta-
waiting
for the Atlantic which drains the mountains with
practiced venom
waiting
for a history which snails towards the coast,
a delta of meandering dreams
waiting
for the bubbles of Bussa
where rock riles river and a conquering boat
fathoms the sand in a tumble of mysty furies
waiting
the Nile knows, the Limpopo lingers,
the Kilimanjaro preserves the lore in icy memory
waiting
> But for how long can the hen wait
> Whose lay is forage for galloping wolves?

Ask Sharpeville
ask Langa
ask Soweto

Where green graves cluster like question marks

Ask Steve
ask Walter
ask Nelson

who seed waiting moments with sinews of fleeting seasons

Ask
    the metaphor of our strength

Ask
    the strength of our metaphor

Ask
    the breaking, broken stones of Robbing Island
    where the ocean's water is sulphur
    where aching walls harbour a dragon
    in every crack

Ask
    the bleeding anthem on the lips of wounded kraals

Ask
    the dappled darings on billowing banners

Dappled
    like the grave where Sankara lies, a waiting eagle,

Dappled
   like the windward dream of Bishop

Dappled
   like the seeing History of Rodney

Ask:
   the stone under Nelson's hammer is bread
   river with faithful wings
   wind the jasmine in its breath;

Ask
   the stone is an ocean
   which cannot count its shoal of eyes

Waiting
   for the kaffir buried four hundred days a year
   in orphaning pits
   for the Boer trapped by the diamond dazzle
   of unanswerable plunderings

Time ambles in diverse paces . . .

XI

Waiting,
still waiting,
like the strident summon of hasty edicts,
bellowed by the smoking lips of vulgar guns,
signed in blood, unleashed in the crimson spine
of trembling streets

And the winds return,
laden with adamantine thou-shalt-nots
of green gods;
a jointless Fear goosesteps the compound of our minds
with epaulettes of night, belts of fuming cobras;
purple swaggers manacle our days
and trees swap their fruits for stony orders

> These are seasons of barking guns
> These are seasons of barking guns;
> They whose ears are close to the earth
> Let them take cover in the bunker of their wits

The lion grows iron-maned and bans the flock
The crocodile turns stone-jawed and bans the shoals

The cloud grows cotton-headed and bans the rain
The valley turns tunnel-hearted and bans the river

The sky grows swollen-headed and bans the sun
The sea turns beady-eyed and bans its salt

The shogun grows cannon-drunk and bans himself
But are these the messiahs
who came four seasons ago
with joyful drums and retinues of chanted pledges?
Where now the aura,
where, the anointed covenant of eloquent knights?

* * *

And bellowed the shogun
with a swaggering viper in his armpit,
a raging geyser in his regimented nose
Bellowed the shogun
with a dusky grain around his lips:

I proscribe	the snail
I proscribe	the shell
I proscribe	the frog
I proscribe	the tadpole
I proscribe	the sea
I proscribe	the sky
I proscribe	the sun
I proscribe	the moon
I proscribe	the tale
I proscribe	the TRUTH
I proscribe	HISTORY!

* * *

The bison who thinks he is the king of the wild
      let him remember raging elephants
         with legs of mortar

The hillock which thinks it is the frontier of heights
      let it remember the Kilimanjaro so hot
         with a peak of simmering snow

The streamlet which thinks it is the Zambesi of the lore
      let it remember the sea which merges earth
         and sky in realms of misty blue

The prophet who thinks he has conquered tomorrow
      let him mount galloping mountains and marvel
         dodging canters of the horse of time

The shogun who says he is an awesome god
      let him take note of burning statues
         and streets wild with vengeful spears . . .

*   *   *

And waiting,
still waiting,
like the mouth for its fiery tongue.

XII

Waiting
       like the pothole for its po(r)tion of blood

       like the smart General for his umpteenth million

       like idle bugs for their nightly feast

       like the prattling tongues of parliaments of ruse

       like Blaise for a trusting Thomas

       like Imelda for her shoes.

XIII

Waiting
        like a hyena
        for the anniversary of its pounce;
        waiting
        like an African despot
        for the seventieth year of his rule.

XIV

Òkerebú kerebú
Kerebú kerebù

And the snake says to the toad;
'I have not had a meal
For a good one week;
And my stomach yearns
For your juicy meat'

'Suppose I turn into a mountain?'
Asks the toad,

'I will level you in the valley
Of my belly'

'Suppose I turn into a river?'

'You will flow easily through
The channels of my mouth'

'Suppose I become one
Of your favourable children?'

'I will eat you
With all the motherly love
In this world'

The toad then turns into a rock
And the snake swallows it
With delicious despatch

Ah! *àràmòndà*[1]
The mouth has swallowed something
Too hard for the mill of the stomach

Òkerebú kerebú
kerebú kerebù

Our tale is a bride
Waiting
For the nimble fancy of the grooming ear.

[1]*àràmòndà*   wonder of wonders!

111

XV

Whoever hasn't kissed the sticky lips
of an envelope,
licked the glossy spine of a stamp,
lacing pigeon winds with syllables
of feathered breaths

Whoever hasn't fondled the legend of the grape
teased the mammary temper of the joyous pawpaw
incited humble carrots to riot,
swollen with the pink bluff
of February's relentless sun

Whoever hasn't trampled the wound of the road
touched sour streets on their bruised elbow
mopped the copper sore of August

Whoever hasn't touched the armpit of the rock
watched care-less boulders tremble
with potent laughter
savoured the jubilant tears of lilting lava

Whoever hasn't seen a caravan of Ways
racing after their dashing Means . . .

Whoever hasn't,

is still waiting.

XVI

Waiting
> like the eternal wisdom of
> *Mosáféjó*[1]
> who gave one daughter
> in marriage to six suitors

[1]*Mosáféjó* I-am-averse-to-litigations

XVII

(sowing)

And when a long-awaited shower
has rid earth's brow
of the debris of sweltering seasons

When heavy clouds have known
their labour, and a steel-handed sun
midwives the mists

in noons of convectional brewings,
rivers learn once more
their liquid lessons, the valley so

       quick with veins of fresh tiding

When a long-awaited shower
has softened the pilgrimage of the dibble,
corn-grains sing their way to germinal roots

of lying ridges. Seedlings dream truant tendrils
in the moistening bed of unpunctual heaps;
the tuber is one patience away,

climbing through stakes
through pinna-leafed groves
through vines which twine the moons

       like wayward pythons

Bent now
the farmer's back;
the hoe's edict chills the spine

of sowing seasons. And the sweat
which rivers down the mountain of the brow,
finds gathering basin at the root of coming harvests

Oh seminal seasons
oh moons of sporing shadows;
laughing barns are just a tear away

and the plenitude which threshes the throes of
                              ripening valleys

XVIII

Waiting
still waiting

Grant us

the fortitude of the lamb which lames a lion-
without inheriting its claws

the daring of the egg which hardens its temple
in a golgotha of breaking shells

the valour of the abyss which hurls its crest
above the conspiracy of severe mountains

the wisdom of seasons which see
the hidden dagger in a plumage of smiles

Grant us

the depth of the sky, height of the sea
fancies which flesh the bones of grating facts

moons which dwell the sky of every brow
on nights when love's labour is never lost.

DATE DUE